JAZZ PIANO SOLOS VOLUME 66

Arranged by Brent Edstrom

contents

ISBN 978-1-70519-332-7

Visit Hal Leonard Online at **www.halleonard.com**

Explore the entire family of Hal Leonard products and resources

World headquarters, contact:
Hal Leonard
7777 West Bluemound Road
Milwaukee, WI 53213
Email: info@halleonard.com

In Europe, contact:
Hal Leonard Europe Limited
1 Red Place
London, W1K 6PL
Email: info@halleonardeurope.com

In Australia, contact:
Hal Leonard Australia Pty. Ltd.
4 Lentara Court
Cheltenham, Victoria, 3192 Australia
Email: info@halleonard.com.au

ALONE TOGETHER

Lyrics by HOWARD DIETZ
Music by ARTHUR SCHWARTZ

4

AUTUMN LEAVES

English lyric by JOHNNY MERCER
French lyric by JACQUES PREVERT
Music by JOSEPH KOSMA

Slowly, with feeling, straight 8ths

BUT BEAUTIFUL

from ROAD TO RIO

Words by JOHNNY BURKE
Music by JIMMY VAN HEUSEN

DON'T EXPLAIN

Words and Music by BILLIE HOLIDAY
and ARTHUR HERZOG

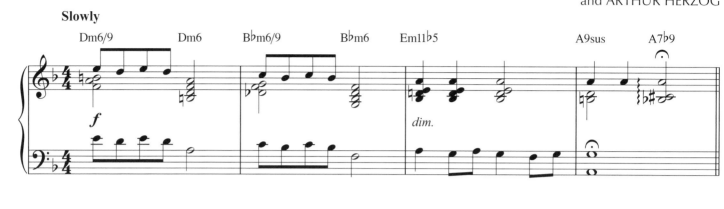

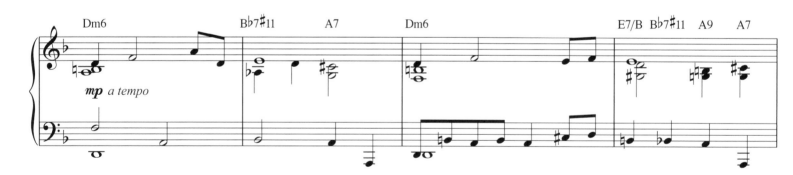

A FLOWER IS A LOVESOME THING

By BILLY STRAYHORN

HARLEM NOCTURNE

Words by EARLE HAGEN
Music by DICK ROGERS

HOW INSENSITIVE
(Insensatez)

Music by ANTONIO CARLOS JOBIM
Original Words by VINICIUS DE MORAES
English Words by NORMAN GIMBEL

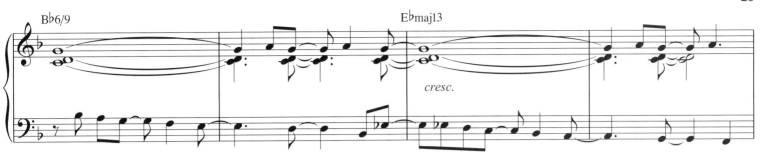

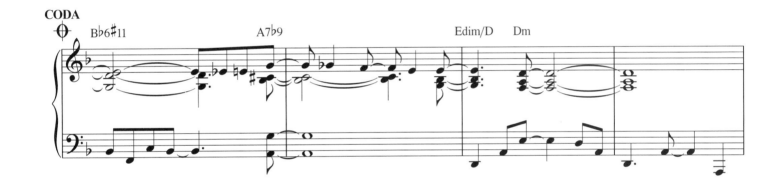

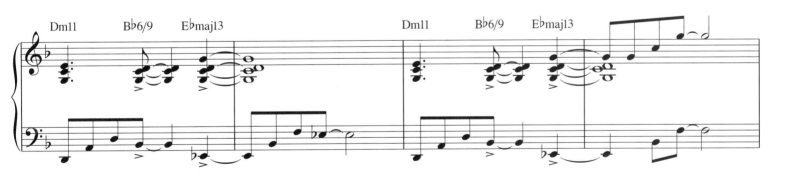

I'LL TAKE ROMANCE

Lyrics by OSCAR HAMMERSTEIN II
Music by BEN OAKLAND

Moderate Swing

IMAGINATION

Words by JOHNNY BURKE
Music by JIMMY VAN HEUSEN

IN A SENTIMENTAL MOOD

By DUKE ELLINGTON

32

IT NEVER ENTERED MY MIND

from HIGHER AND HIGHER

Words by LORENZ HART
Music by RICHARD RODGERS

MOON RIVER

from the Paramount Picture BREAKFAST AT TIFFANY'S

Words by JOHNNY MERCER
Music by HENRY MANCINI

38

IT'S ALWAYS YOU
from the Paramount Picture ROAD TO ZANZIBAR

Words by JOHNNY BURKE
Music by JAMES VAN HEUSEN

MY FOOLISH HEART

from MY FOOLISH HEART

Words by NED WASHINGTON
Music by VICTOR YOUNG

Slowly and expressively, straight 8ths

QUIET NIGHTS OF QUIET STARS
(Corcovado)

English Words by GENE LEES
Original Words and Music by
ANTONIO CARLOS JOBIM

48

MY HEART STOOD STILL

from A CONNECTICUT YANKEE

Words by LORENZ HART
Music by RICHARD RODGERS

PRELUDE TO A KISS

Words by IRVING GORDON
and IRVING MILLS
Music by DUKE ELLINGTON

Tender Ballad, straight 8ths

PURE IMAGINATION
from WILLY WONKA AND THE CHOCOLATE FACTORY

Words and Music by LESLIE BRICUSSE
and ANTHONY NEWLEY

SAY IT
(Over and Over Again)

Words by FRANK LOESSER
and JIMMY McHUGH
Music by JIMMY McHUGH

64

SOLITUDE

Words and Music by DUKE ELLINGTON,
EDDIE De LANGE and IRVING MILLE

SWEET AND LOVELY

Words and Music by GUS ARNHEIM,
CHARLES N. DANIELS and HARRY TOBIAS

THE VERY THOUGHT OF YOU

Words and Music by
RAY NOBLE

With a slow, easy Swing 8ths

74

WHEN I FALL IN LOVE

from ONE MINUTE TO ZERO

Words by EDWARD HEYMAN
Music by VICTOR YOUNG

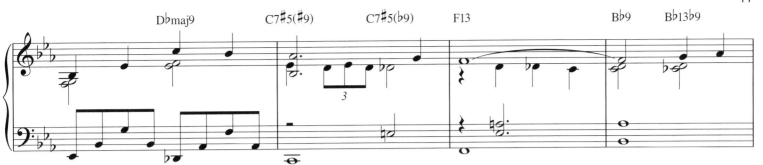

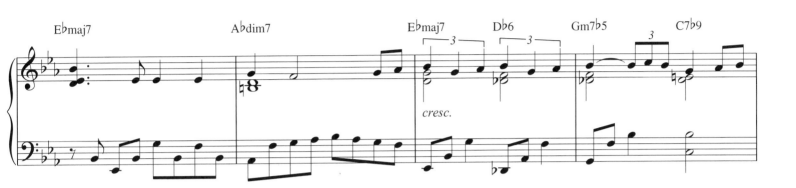

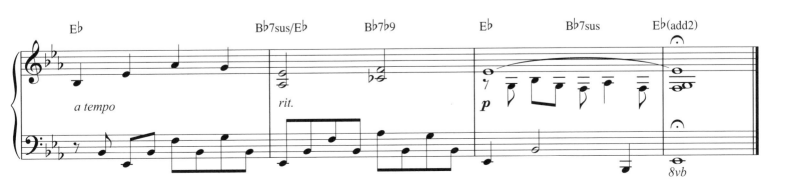

WHEN YOUR LOVER HAS GONE

Words and Music by
E.A. SWAN